SHARKS!

LORI STEIN

SHARKS!

Published by Liberty Street,
an imprint of Time Inc. Books
225 Liberty Street
New York, New York 10281

LIBERTY
STREET

LIBERTY STREET is a trademark of Time Inc.

Hardcover edition
ISBN 10: 1-61893-184-9
ISBN 13: 978-1-61893-184-9
Library of Congress Control Number: 2016939086

First edition, 2016

1 QGT 16

10 9 8 7 6 5 4 3 2 1

Some of the content in this book was originally published in *Discovery Sharkopedia: The Complete Guide to Everything Shark.*

Produced by Scout Books & Media Inc

Time Inc. Books products may be purchased for business or promotional use. For information on bulk purchases, please contact Christi Crowley in the Special Sales Department at (845) 895-9858.

To order Time Inc. Books Collector's Editions, please call (800) 327-6388, Monday through Friday, 7 a.m.–9 p.m., Central Time.

We welcome your comments and suggestions about Time Inc. Books. Please write to us at: Time Inc. Books, Attention: Book Editors, P.O. Box 62310, Tampa, Florida 33662–2310.

timeincbooks.com

Scientists have divided all the sharks in the world into eight orders. The sharks within each order have some similar features. Sharks whose names are listed in **bold** appear in Meet the Shark Orders on page 110, under the name of the order they belong to.

CONTENTS

Shark Bite: THE BODY OF THE BEAST 4

Chapter 1: WHAT MAKES A SHARK A SHARK? 7

Chapter 2: SENSATIONAL SENSES 17

Chapter 3: GREAT WHITES: THE FIERCEST HUNTERS 27

Chapter 4: WHAT'S FOR DINNER? 37

Chapter 5: TRICKY SHARKS 47

Chapter 6: GROWING UP SHARK 59

Shark Bite: EXTREME SHARKS 66

Chapter 7: OCEAN ODDBALLS 69

Chapter 8: SMART SHARKS 79

Chapter 9: IT'S A SHARK'S LIFE 87

Chapter 10: A SHARK BITE STORY 95

Chapter 11: WHY SHARKS MATTER 103

Resources   108

Meet the Shark Orders   110

Index   111

Credits and Acknowledgments   112

THE BODY OF THE BEAST

Different sharks have different bodies, but most have the same features. Here is how those features look on a **Caribbean reef shark.**

Caudal fin

Anal fin

Pelvic fin

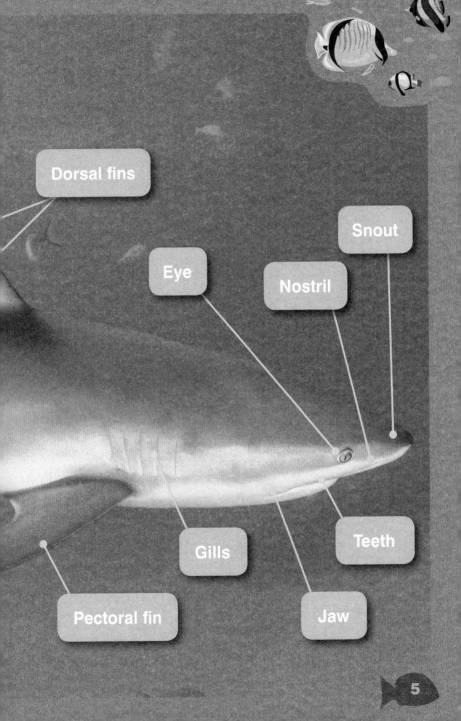

Dorsal fins

Snout

Eye

Nostril

Gills

Pectoral fin

Jaw

Teeth

BIG AND BOLD Tiger sharks have wide heads and bodies that get thinner near the tail. Their tigerlike stripes fade as they get older.

CHAPTER 1

WHAT MAKES A SHARK A SHARK?

There are nearly 500 different species of sharks swimming in oceans around the world. Sharks don't all look the same. They come in many sizes, shapes, and colors. They don't act the same. Some are gentle and slow, some are fierce and fast. They don't all live in the same kind of place or eat the same food. They don't hunt, breathe, or have babies the same way. So what makes a fish a shark?

All sharks share many useful features.

Sharks don't have bones. Their skeletons are made of a tough material that can bend easily. It is called cartilage (CAHR-teh-lij). This material is lighter than bone, so sharks' bodies are light. This means they use less energy moving through the water. If they stopped swimming, they would sink. Cartilage lets sharks twist their bodies. This helps them catch prey (the animals they eat).

Most fish have scales on their bodies, but not sharks. Their skin is covered with hard bumps called denticles. This makes their skin strong and hard to tear.

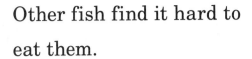

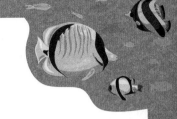

Other fish find it hard to
eat them.

Sharks have powerful jaws.
(Jaws are the lower part of the face
where teeth are found.) Shark jaws
are not attached to the skull. The
fish can push their jaws forward to
catch prey. Inside those powerful
jaws, all sharks have teeth. Some
have hundreds of tiny teeth. Some
have big, jagged teeth for ripping food
apart. Most sharks have 5 to 15 rows
of teeth.

Like all fish, sharks breathe
through the gills on the sides of their
heads. The gills pull oxygen from the
water around them. But while most
fish have one gill on each side of the

GILLS are long slits on on each side of the head.

head, sharks have five to seven pairs of gills.

All sharks have fins. They have one or two dorsal (back) fins, a caudal (tail) fin, and a pectoral (chest) fin. Sharks use their fins to move through the water. Some sharks have huge, well-developed fins, and some have smaller ones. Sharks that swim in open waters, such as **oceanic whitetip sharks,** have large,

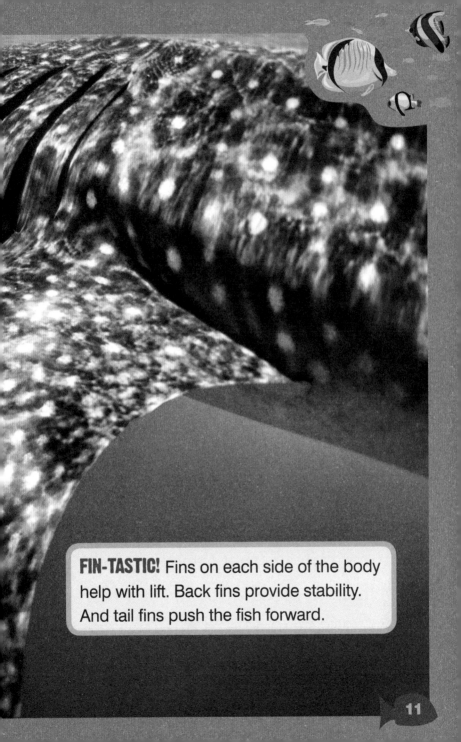

FIN-TASTIC! Fins on each side of the body help with lift. Back fins provide stability. And tail fins push the fish forward.

IS THE DOCTOR IN?

SHARKS HELP PEOPLE

Like other animals, sharks get viruses and cancers. But they don't get sick as often. Scientists are studying sharks to see why they fight disease so well. A study at the Georgetown University Medical Center found that squalamine (SKWUH-luh-meen), which is found in **dogfish sharks**, may kill some viruses that also attack humans.

strong fins that help them swim long distances. Those that mostly rest on the ocean floor, such as **nurse sharks**, have smaller, weaker fins. The fastest sharks, such as **salmon sharks**, have strong tail fins that they move back and forth to speed through the water.

Despite all the things sharks have in common, there are

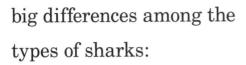

big differences among the
types of sharks:

- Heavy, tough **bull sharks**
  have poor eyesight. They stun
  their prey by bumping it with
  their massive snouts (nose and
  mouth areas).

- Tiger sharks are named for the
  stripes on their backs. They are
  among the biggest eaters in the
  ocean. They are sometimes called
  "garbage guts" because they will
  taste almost anything to see if it's
  food, including car parts and glass
  bottles.

- **Mako sharks** have shiny blue skin
  and slender bodies. They zip through
  the water with lightning speed.

FACT FILE: MANY DIFFERENCES

Sharks share many similar features, but that doesn't stop them from looking different.

Sharks can be as small as a 7-inch **dwarf lantern shark** and as big as a 40-foot **whale shark.**

Makos are blue and shiny like metal.

Lemon sharks are sandy yellow.

Zebra sharks have bold patterns in pale yellow with black spots.

Great white sharks are long, with round bodies.

Angelsharks look flat.

The eyes of **hammerhead sharks** are on each end of a wide, flat head.

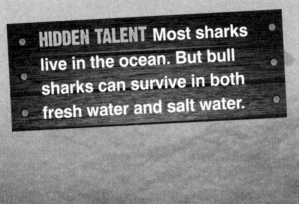

HIDDEN TALENT Most sharks live in the ocean. But bull sharks can survive in both fresh water and salt water.

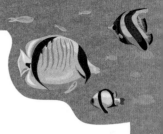

SENSATIONAL SENSES

Sharks have the same five senses people have—smell, vision, hearing, taste, and touch. They also have amazing extra senses. One of their most useful extra senses is electroreception (ih-LEK-trow-rih-SEP-shun), the ability to receive, or sense, the electrical signals that all animals send out. This helps them find prey in dark water. Sharks can also sense vibrations and changes in water pressure. All these senses give sharks super powers for hunting and survival.

Sharks have an amazing sense of smell. Two-thirds of a shark's brain is used to process smells. A shark can smell a tiny bit of blood or guts from far away. How does this work? A shark's nostrils are under its head. Water passes over the shark's snout, through the nostrils, and over the shark's smell sensors.

If a shark smells prey or food, it will follow the scent. It can tell if the scent is coming from the right or left nostril. As the shark gets closer to its prey, the scent gets stronger.

Most sharks have good eyesight. Deep-sea sharks usually

have large, light-colored eyes. These let in enough light for them to see in the dark water where they live. Sharks that swim nearer the surface have eyes that are darker and smaller to protect them from bright sunlight at the surface.

HOW DO SHARKS SEE IN DARK OCEAN WATER?

Many sharks have eyes similar to a cat. A mirrorlike layer in the back reflects more light through the eye. This helps them to see better in low light.

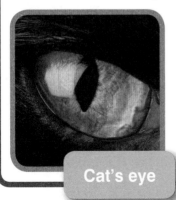

Cat's eye

Catshark's eye

Sharks' eyes are similar to humans'. The irises and pupils get bigger or smaller to control the amount of light that gets in. Sharks' eyes have lenses that help them focus. But they can't see things far away. They find and follow their prey by smelling its scent and feeling its vibrations. When they get close—about 100 feet away—they can see it.

Sharks' ears are inside their heads. The only visible parts are two small holes. These holes lead to tubes filled with fluid. The fluid is good at carrying sound. Sharks can hear very low sounds—the kind that carry well through ocean waters. Sharks can hear fish moving in

the water. They also hear changes in water currents.

When do sharks rely on their sense of touch? When they are curious about a thing and want to see what it is, sharks may bump it with their snouts. They also have touch sensors all over their bodies that can feel changes in water pressure and water temperature. This alerts them to danger. It also lets them know when to move to cooler or warmer waters.

Sharks have taste buds in their mouths, but not on their tongues (where humans' taste buds are located). Experts think sharks use their sense of taste to find out what food is good to eat. When a shark

LATERAL LINES are a series of tubes that run along a shark's body. They are shown here traced in red. These sense organs feel vibrations and changes in water pressure. This tells the shark that other animals are swimming nearby.

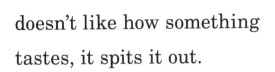

doesn't like how something tastes, it spits it out.

Sharks use one of their special senses, electroreception, to pick up electrical signals when searching for food. They detect these electrical signals through gel-filled pores on their heads. The pores are called the ampullae (am-PULL-ee) of Lorenzini. (Ampullae are little sacs. They were discovered by a scientist named Stefano Lorenzini.) Only sharks and rays have these. This sense works only at short distances. It helps sharks find prey that is hidden, such as a fish under the sand.

Marine biologists are scientists who study life in the oceans. They have known for a long time that sharks use their sense of smell to find prey. But they didn't know whether sharks also use smell to find their way home after long trips.

A group of marine biologists decided to test how well sharks found their way home when they could not smell. The scientists worked at Scripps Institution of Oceanography and the Birch Aquarium in La Jolla, California.

Every year **leopard sharks** gather near the shore of La Jolla before they give birth. So the scientists caught 26 leopard sharks and took them by boat several miles away.

Before they let the sharks go, the scientists blocked the nostrils of 11 of them with cotton balls and petroleum jelly. This didn't last long or hurt the sharks. The 15 sharks with unblocked noses found their way back to the shore with no problem. The 11 who could not smell just wandered around while their noses were blocked.

Marine biologists are not sure what the sharks smell that helps them find their way. It could be the water itself, or the animals that swim in the water. It could be a combination of many things. More research is needed.

Leopard shark

BIG AND POWERFUL Great white sharks are big, fast, and bite with strong jaws.

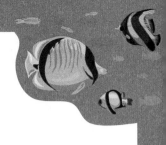

GREAT WHITES: THE FIERCEST HUNTERS

Great white sharks are not the biggest or the fastest sharks in the world. But they are the most well known. They are not the most deadly sharks in the ocean, but people think they are. This is because of how they have been shown in movies and stories. But it is also because great whites are among the few types of sharks that cause the most bites on people. All sharks eat to live, and great whites are expert hunters. Their vision and sense of smell are better than most sharks. They are fast, intelligent, and super strong.

The great white shark has several features that help it survive. First, its body is shaped like a torpedo, which allows it to move through the water quickly. Its body temperature can vary, so it can swim in warmer and cooler waters.

The great white isn't really white. Its skin is gray on top and white underneath. Seen from above, it blends in with the ocean floor. Seen from below,

SKIN IN THE GAME Sharks have bumps all over their bodies. These are called denticles, which means "small tooth." The denticles are covered with enamel—the same hard coating found on shark and human teeth.

Great white shark

Great white shark tooth

it blends in with the sunlit surface of the ocean. This coloring is called countershading. It helps the shark sneak up on prey.

Great whites have several rows of teeth, and each tooth is about 2 inches long. Those teeth have jagged edges, like a saw.

They are good for catching, cutting, and ripping flesh. A great white's stomach digests food efficiently, so it can get the energy it needs to swim for long distances. It can attack with speed and strength.

The great white has excellent vision. Its eyes are five times bigger than human eyes. The eyes have a layer of crystals that magnify and focus everything the shark sees.

HOW FIERCE IS A GREAT WHITE'S BITE?

Scientists estimate this shark bites with a force of 4,000 pounds per square inch— 20 times the force of a human bite. It is the strongest bite of any living animal.

(Magnifying makes things appear larger. Focusing makes them appear clearer.) Great whites move their pupils and other eye parts around to protect them when they attack prey.

The great white shark has a great sense of smell, too. Its olfactory bulb (the place where the nerves for smelling begin) is larger than it is in other sharks. This shark can smell just one drop of blood in 10 billion drops of water.

The great white's size, speed, powerful jaws, and excellent senses make it a top predator (an animal that isn't prey for other animals). In the ocean, sharks are top predators, and great whites are the top predators of the shark world.

IN YOUR NEWSFEED

TAG, YOU'RE IT!

HERE COMES MARY LEE

When Mary Lee is coming, everyone knows to head for the shore. Mary Lee is a great white who was tagged with a radio transmitter while she was in Cape Cod, Massachusetts. (The research program director named the shark after her mother.) Scientists wanted to find out where Mary Lee goes every winter. It turns out she goes south, to Florida. Sometimes the group gets a radio signal that tells them Mary Lee is swimming by a beach used by people. They notify officials near that beach to get everyone out of the water. You can follow her journey at this website: ocearch.org/profile/mary_lee/.

FACT FILE: JUMPING SHARKS!

One way a great white hunts is by swimming up under its prey and grabbing it. When it does this, it leaps from the ocean, splits the water, and thrusts its body into the air. This is called breaching, and is mostly seen in great white sharks off the coast of South Africa. In that region, the ocean is shallow, so great whites can cruise along the bottom and thrust upward when they see or sense prey, usually seals or sea lions.

How do sharks make this dramatic leap? First, they pick up speed as they move up from about 100 feet deep. By the time they are under a seal, they are moving at around 20 miles per hour. The shark hits the seal with the same force as a car crash. Scientists believe the seal is stunned or possibly dead from the force of the blow before it is eaten by the great white.

Seal Island, off the coast of Cape Town, South Africa, is home to large colonies of Cape fur seals. Great whites have a special technique for catching them. The sharks swim in a circle around the island. When a seal swims off the island to find food in the open water, a shark will swoop under it, breach, and catch it. Sometimes the seal gets away.

Great white shark breaching

FEEDING FRENZY! A feeding frenzy can occur when a shark sees that another shark has found something good to eat and joins in. As more and more sharks join the group, it turns from a feast into a fight. Some feeding frenzies involve hundreds of sharks fighting over the same food.

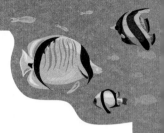

WHAT'S FOR DINNER?

Food gives sharks the energy they need to swim around all day and night. It's hard to find food in the big ocean, but sharks are successful hunters. They are experts at choosing the right food, finding it, catching it, and eating it. Their teeth, jaws, ways of hunting, and digestive systems help them survive.

What's on the menu? Sharks eat a variety of foods, but all sharks are carnivores. They eat meat. Some people think sharks will eat anything, but sharks are actually picky eaters. Some live where there is plenty of food. Others roam the oceans hunting for the food that's best for them.

Usually, bigger sharks look for bigger prey. But the largest shark in the ocean eats some of the smallest creatures. Whale sharks eat zooplankton (ZOH-uh-PLANK-tuhn), which includes tiny fish, jellyfish, and fish eggs. How does such a big animal eat such tiny things? A hungry whale shark can open its mouth wide and gulp large mouthfuls of water. The water is full of zooplankton. Or it swims

TINY TEETH CALLED GILL RAKERS help whale sharks filter food from the seawater.

forward and lets the water pass over its gills. It has a built-in filter system to separate out the food from the water. The water passes through the filter and returns to the ocean. The whale shark swallows the food left behind.

Many small sharks, such as **blue sharks**, feast on squid, octopus, and cuttlefish. Some sharks, like **bullhead sharks**, have special teeth that can crunch through hard shells. They eat animals like lobsters, crabs, and clams. Bigger sharks, such as makos, eat bigger fish, such as bluefish and tuna. They also eat smaller sharks. Big sharks, such as great whites, eat seals, sea lions, seabirds, and turtles. They have sharp, pointy teeth with jagged edges designed to tear their food into bite-size pieces.

Sharks have teeth designed for the food they eat. They can have anywhere from two to as many as 50 rows of teeth, depending on the species (type of shark). The teeth don't have roots, so they fall out easily. But sharks have a unique tooth replacement system. When a tooth falls out, another one moves up from the row behind to take its place. This can happen in as little as a day or two.

Rows of teeth

Sharks can't chew their food. They can push their entire jaws out to catch food. But they can't easily move the lower part of their jaw separately from the upper part in order to chew. Instead, sharks catch prey in their strong jaws and use their sharp teeth to tear it into pieces. The pieces are small enough to swallow. Some sharks, such as nurse sharks, can use their mouths like a vacuum cleaner to suck in food. Some shake their heads to break the food into easy-to-swallow pieces.

What happens to the food once a shark swallows it? Most sharks digest food slowly. If they eat something they can't digest, they throw it up. They have special valve systems that keep food moving slowly through their digestive systems. This helps sharks get more nutrients from their food. This process can take two or three days for larger sharks.

Also, a shark's stomach can expand (get bigger). This means a shark can eat bigger meals that give them energy for longer. This way, the shark has a ready supply of food to give it the energy it needs to hunt again.

WHAT HAPPENS TO LOST SHARK TEETH?

A shark can grow, lose, and regrow up to 50,000 teeth in its lifetime. When a tooth falls out, it falls to the bottom of the ocean and becomes a fossil. Sometimes these fossils are carried to shore by the tide or found by scuba divers.

FACT FILE: HUNTING HABITS

Sharks have super-useful skills that they use to catch and eat prey.

Speed Sharks are fast. Some swim up to 30 miles per hour or faster and can outswim most of the fastest fish. The **shortfin mako** has been measured swimming at a speed of 40 miles per hour. It is one of the few fish that can swim fast enough to catch a bluefin tuna.

Shortfin mako

Ambush Sharks can camouflage (hide) themselves on the ocean bottom and stay still for hours or days. When a smaller animal comes near, they pounce.

Tasselled wobbegong

Deception Tiger sharks have been observed swimming quietly past prey, allowing the other fish to feel safe. Then they turn back and attack.

Strength Bull sharks are not subtle at all. They use their keen sense of smell to sniff out prey; then they head-butt it to stun it before chomping down. This is called bump and bite.

FACE TIME! Nurse sharks hang out in groups. These slow movers are sometimes called the "couch potatoes" of the shark world.

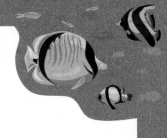

TRICKY SHARKS

Some sharks are huge, fierce fish that are feared by all the other animals in the water. But most sharks are less than 6 feet long.

Smaller sharks need big tricks to help them hunt and survive. Some may find safety—and food—in a large crowd. Others hide—and hunt—in plain sight. Some can make themselves bigger or smaller to avoid being eaten.

The **spiny dogfish shark** is just 3 feet long. That means it's small enough to be a meal for other sharks. When it sees larger sharks nearby, it curls up and points its sharp tail at them to scare them away. This small shark finds safety in numbers, too. Males join groups, called packs, of hundreds of spiny dogfish. They protect each other and hunt together.

Also known as a sand devil, the angelshark behaves more like a devil.

A spiny dogfish shark

Its skin colors and patterns match the ocean floor. It blends in and is hard to see. When prey comes near, the shark pounces, opening its powerful jaws to capture a meal. The angelshark's strong jaws, sharp teeth, and the element of surprise are on its side. The small fish and shellfish that it eats don't have a chance of escaping.

This sneaky fish has another trick to stay hidden as it waits for prey. It uses the strong muscles in its fins to dig into sand and mud and bury itself. Only the eyes and the top of its body can be seen. The angelshark can stay that way for days, waiting for something yummy to swim by.

SURPRISE! The angelshark is an ambush predator. It hides and then surprises its prey. It takes only about one-tenth of a second for an angelshark to pop up and snatch prey.

There are more than 150 different kinds of **catsharks**. They are small, ranging from 2 to 5 feet long. Catsharks have beautiful, catlike eyes. When frightened by predators, catsharks have many ways of protecting themselves.

The **swell shark**, a type of catshark, has a nifty way of staying alive—it swells up. When it sees a predator approaching, it grabs its tail fins with its teeth, forming a U-shape. Then it

GOT AIR?

A swell shark doesn't need water to swell up. It can swallow air to double in size. When the swell shark expels the air, it makes a sound like a dog's bark.

SALMON SHARK

NEW SPEED RECORD

The US Navy has recorded salmon sharks swimming at 55 miles per hour. This beats the previous record holder, the shortfin mako shark. Salmon sharks move their tails back and forth quickly while holding their bodies mostly straight. This allows them to move fast in a straight line.

swallows water until it balloons up to double its size. This makes the small shark look bigger and scarier. Predators may think they can't win a fight and turn away.

The **puffadder shyshark** has a special trick to avoid being eaten by a hungry fur seal. It curls up into a tight ball and covers its eyes with its tail. Scientists think this makes the shark harder to swallow, so predators leave it alone. Other catsharks, including **pajama sharks** and **leopard catsharks**, also do this.

When a **spinner shark** finds a school of small fish, it charges up through the school, snapping on all sides until it catches a fish. It swallows the fish whole. Spinner shark teeth are perfect for catching fish. They are not a good shape for tearing it into bite-size pieces. When a spinner shark moves upward to catch a fish, it may jump right out of the water. It spins through the air, making three of four turns before diving back down.

The **thresher shark** has a huge tail that is a powerful tool. When a thresher finds a school of fish, such as tuna or mackerel, it whips its long tail around. First it stuns and traps the fish, then it begins to eat.

Thresher shark

TALE OF THE TAIL A thresher's tail can grow to half its body length and a third of its weight. That's big!

Sharks breathe by taking in oxygen from the water that passes over their gills. Many sharks have to swim constantly or they won't be able to breathe. That takes a lot of energy.

Some sharks have a less exhausting way of getting water to pass over their gills. They have strong cheek muscles. They can hold water in their cheeks and then pump the water over their gills. These sharks, including wobbegongs, angelsharks, and nurse sharks, can rest on the ocean floor for a long time without swimming. This trick is called cheek breathing.

About 60 years ago, a Mexican fisherman discovered an underwater cave where the water current is very strong. The cave is near Isla Mujeres, an island off the coast of Mexico. Sharks had discovered the cave, too. The sharks could rest, even sleep, in the cave because the current moved over their gills. They did not have to keep moving. This made the sharks drowsy and calm. Divers visit the cave to see the sharks sleeping with their eyes open. Sometimes, as many as 30 sharks can be found snoozing in the cave. Divers can swim right up to the sharks and even touch them while they sleep.

Nurse shark napping in a cave

MAKE YOUR CASE Some sharks lay eggs. They are in egg cases that protect them before they hatch.

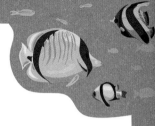

GROWING UP SHARK

Some sharks start out in egg cases. When the egg has developed into a baby shark, the egg case breaks open and the baby shark emerges. This is called hatching. (Birds hatch from eggs, too.) Other baby sharks are born from their mother's body. This is called live birth. Baby sharks are called pups.

Female sharks don't take care of their young the way mammal mothers do. They swim out to sea after the pups are born. Shark pups are able to take care of themselves right away. During the first few years of life, pups grow to their full size. They learn how to hunt and protect themselves. Baby sharks are born with the skills they need to become adults and have babies of their own.

Shark mothers have ways of helping their pups survive and grow. They are careful about where they lay eggs or give birth. Bullhead sharks, for example, lay their eggs in safe places. And tiger shark females give birth in coves and near rivers where the pups may be protected from the dangers of the open ocean.

HOW ARE SHARK PUPS BORN?

LEMON SHARK pups grow inside the female shark until they are ready to be born.

HORN SHARKS lay eggs in protected cases outside their bodies. There is usually one pup in each egg case, but a female shark can lay dozens or even hundreds of eggs.

DOGFISH SHARKS carry eggs inside their bodies; the pups hatch inside the mother's body, then are born.

All shark pups are born underwater and can swim right away.

Experts have learned many things about how shark pups begin their lives. For example, female horn sharks carefully position their egg cases in safe places. The eggs get nourishment inside the cases while they grow. When the pups hatch, they can survive for a month before they need to start eating. After that, they start eating on their own. They choose easy prey, like small shrimp and sea worms.

Bamboo sharks are hatched from eggs in cases that settle on the ocean floor. The pups are 5 to 7 inches long when they're born.

Sixgill shark litters of 22 to 106 pups have been

recorded. That's a lot of brothers and sisters!

All shark pups start life with some survival skills. They don't need to hunt for food for the first few weeks of their lives. Shark pups have sharp teeth, and the ability to use them. They don't have full biting power until they are adults. That's because the cartilage that holds their jaws in place isn't hard enough for a strong bite. It hardens as they grow up. When young sharks try to eat big prey, they can't bite through it. Smaller fish are easier meals for them.

A shark pup looks like a tasty snack for larger fish. How does it survive when it is small and alone? Some young sharks stick together. Some stay close to where they were born for a few years. Then they set off on their own. Pups may stay in shallow water and safer areas such as coves. These places are sometimes called shark nurseries.

All sharks are considered adults when they are able to have babies. Different shark species reach adulthood at different ages. **Smoothhound sharks** can have babies when they are two or three years old. For whale sharks, it may take 30 years. In many species the males and females become adults at different ages.

We don't know exactly how long sharks live. But scientists do know that sharks live long lives and have a variety of life spans. Scientists have estimated life spans for some species.

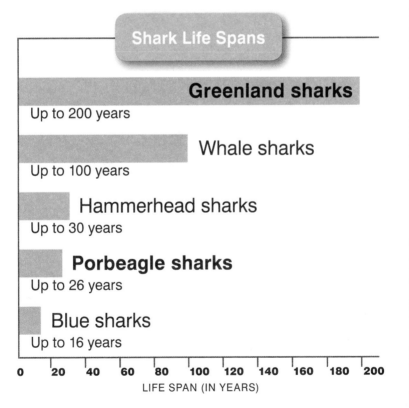

Shark Life Spans

Greenland sharks
Up to 200 years

Whale sharks
Up to 100 years

Hammerhead sharks
Up to 30 years

Porbeagle sharks
Up to 26 years

Blue sharks
Up to 16 years

0   20   40   60   80   100   120   140   160   180   200
LIFE SPAN (IN YEARS)

SHARK BITE

EXTREME SHARKS

SOME OF THE WORLD'S BIGGEST SHARKS

Whale shark
Maximum: 45 feet;
Average: 23 feet

Greenland shark
Maximum: 22 feet;
Average: 11 feet

Great white shark
Maximum: 20 feet;
Average: 14 feet

**Common thresher
shark**
Maximum: 20 feet;
Average: 11 feet

Great hammerhead
Maximum: 19 feet;
Average: 9 feet

Whale shark

Greenland shark

Great white shark

Common thresher shark

Great hammerhead

SOME OF THE WORLD'S SMALLEST SHARKS

Dwarf lanternshark
Average: 8 inches

Pale catshark
Average: 8 inches

Smalleye pygmy shark
Average: 9 inches

Panama ghost catshark
Average: 9 inches

Green lanternshark
Average: 9 inches

DOUBLE-EDGED SAW Odd-looking **sawsharks** use their sawlike snout to kill, shred, and eat prey.

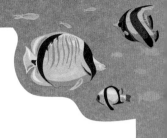

OCEAN ODDBALLS

Some sharks have unusual bodies with frills, horns, or super long whiskers. One shark has a big spike on its head. There are sharks that look like snakes. Others look like old-fashioned rugs. Many sharks have patterns on their skin—stripes, dots, or other markings. These help them hide. And some sharks can light up like a flashlight.

Bamboo sharks have slender bodies. Most are less than 3 feet long. Their thick tails are often as long as their bodies. Bamboo sharks are not aggressive. Their patterned skin helps them blend in, making it hard for prey to see them coming. Predators that hunt bamboo sharks can't easily spot them.

A brown-banded bamboo shark

Wobbegong live on sandy ledges or the floor of the ocean. They have shaggy or lacey whiskerlike growths called barbels. These barbels are very sensitive. Wobbegongs use them to feel their way along the ocean floor.

The wobbegong blends into its habitat.

Frilled sharks have long, narrow bodies. Their mouths are big and are filled with sharp teeth. They look a bit like mouths with tails. They are named for the frills over the gills on the sides of their heads.

Bullhead and horn sharks are slow and tend to stay in one place. This could

A crested horn shark

make them look like easy prey for others. But when a predator chomps down, it finds a painful surprise. These sharks have sharp horns and venomous spines. The predator may stop biting long enough for the shark to get away.

Most **lantern sharks** carry their own light sources. Like glowworms and fireflies, they have organs called photophores (FOH-tow-fohrz) that glow when needed. Lantern sharks live in deep, dark waters. Having their own light is helpful when they need to see prey or attract a mate. The ability to make their own light is called bioluminescence—a long word that means "living light."

NINJA LANTERNSHARKS

DEEP SEA DISCOVERY

In December, 2015, a new shark species was named by scientists. The 18-inch-long shark has a solid black body that blends in with the deep ocean where it lives. Its name is **ninja lanternshark**. In Japanese folklore, ninjas were often described as silent warriors dressed in black.

The **goblin shark** has been called the ugliest living shark. It has a long, pointed snout, which it uses to dig for shellfish on the ocean floor. Its mouth is filled with needle-sharp teeth that it uses to spear and then tear its prey. When it attacks prey, it pushes its whole jaw out of its mouth. When it's finished eating, it pulls its jaw back in.

A basking shark

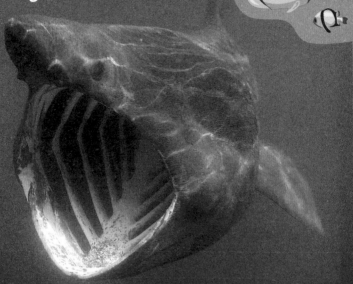

Basking sharks are enormous. They can be up to 30 feet long and weigh 40,000 pounds. They have a huge mouth, which stays open most of the time. As they swim slowly, small fish and zooplankton enter their open mouths. The basking shark's tiny teeth separate the water from the fish. They spit out the water and eat the fish.

FACT FILE: DEEP-SEA DISCOVERY

Many of the oddest sharks in the world live more than a mile under the surface. This is the deepest part of the ocean. Scientists look for new ways to explore these deep waters. They develop better submersibles (underwater vehicles used to dive into the deepest parts of the ocean). And they find new ways to analyze the information they gather. These things have helped scientists discover new shark species.

John McCosker, chairman of aquatic biology at the California Academy of Sciences, was on a research mission near the Galápagos Islands. He was in an underwater vehicle called a submersible. He looked out the window and saw a shark that looked different from any he had seen before. The dark brown shark had light, oddly shaped spots scattered over its body. This was unusual. He thought it was a new species.

When McCosker got back to shore, he wrote a detailed description of the shark. He pointed out the unusual color and pattern, its sharp teeth, its body size, and where its fins were positioned. And he wrote where he had found it. It took many years to confirm his find. McCosker had discovered a brand-new species, and it was named the **Galápagos catshark**.

Scientists travel to the deepest parts of the ocean in submersible vessels such as this one to find and study deep-sea sharks.

HEAD OF THE CLASS
Hammerheads have an enormous mouth under a huge T-shaped head. The mouth looks small compared to the size of the head.

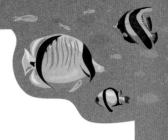

CHAPTER 8

SMART SHARKS

Hammerheads are weird-looking creatures. They have long, narrow, hammer-shaped heads, with eyes at either end. When they swim through the ocean, hammerheads move their heads from side to side. Some scientists think this motion helps them see better. Or it may help them keep their balance or pick up electrical signals from other creatures.

Hammerheads are called "smart sharks" because they use their heads to be better hunters. Their eyes are spaced far apart. This helps them see in front of them and also far to the sides. They can see all the creatures swimming around them. And they have good depth perception—they can see how near or far away things are. They have lots of ampullae of Lorenzini on their wide heads. The tiny sense organs receive the electrical signals all living creatures give off.

There are nine different species, or types, of hammerheads. They swim in warm waters all over the world. **Scalloped hammerheads** are the most common species.

HAMMERHEAD SHAPES

There are nine species in the hammerhead group. Each species has a slightly different head shape, with different creases and bumps. The names of the species describe these features.

Scalloped

Bonnethead

Smooth

NAME GAME A group of hammerhead sharks is called a school, a shoal, or a shiver.

WHERE'S THE GOOD STUFF?

LOOKING FOR FOOD

In 2014, scientists attached a tracking device to a young hammerhead shark. They followed him for ten months. They discovered that sometimes the shark swam in a large school near the coast. But other times it moved to deeper waters to find more fish to eat.

Female scalloped hammerheads grow to about 8 feet long; males are smaller, usually less than 6 feet.

Each school of hammerheads forms a community. The largest sharks swim near the center of the pack and younger ones swim on the outside.

No one is sure why hammerheads form groups—many other

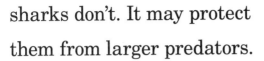

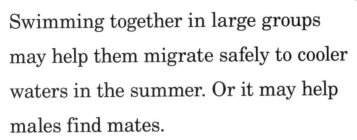

sharks don't. It may protect them from larger predators. Swimming together in large groups may help them migrate safely to cooler waters in the summer. Or it may help males find mates.

Scalloped hammerheads are social and hang around in groups called schools. Hundreds of them swim together.

Great hammerheads are the biggest members of the hammerhead group. They are also one of the ten biggest sharks in the world. They are good hunters, but they rarely attack people. Divers have reported that great hammerheads sometimes seem curious and swim around them. When the divers try to approach, the big sharks swim away.

GOING MY WAY? Small fish called remoras sometimes attach themselves to sharks' bodies. The sharks allow them to hang on.

CHAPTER 9

IT'S A SHARK'S LIFE

There are two main things sharks do: breathe and eat. To breathe, many sharks need to keep swimming so that water passes over their gills. To eat, they have to hunt and kill their prey. These activities keep them busy. But researchers have discovered other things sharks do.

Sharks sometimes slap their fins against the water. This is called fin flapping. And sharks sometimes browse, checking out their surroundings.

Sharks swim to breathe and hunt. But sometimes they seem to be checking out the scenery as well. Underwater photographers say sharks swim up and check out their camera equipment. This might be because the cameras give off electrical signals and the sharks think they are food. But many divers report that sharks seem genuinely curious.

Some sharks use their bodies for communicating with other sharks. Great

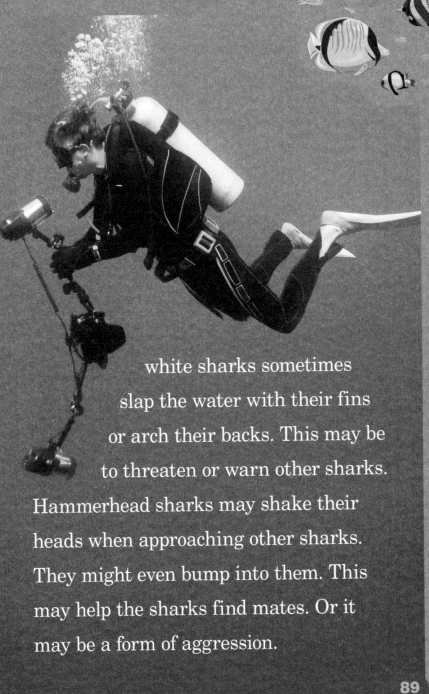

white sharks sometimes
slap the water with their fins
or arch their backs. This may be
to threaten or warn other sharks.
Hammerhead sharks may shake their
heads when approaching other sharks.
They might even bump into them. This
may help the sharks find mates. Or it
may be a form of aggression.

SOCIAL SHARKS

Many sharks are loners, but some are social. Groups of **sevengill sharks** feed at the same time without bothering one another. And occasionally different shark species hang out together—oceanic whitetip sharks are often seen with **silky sharks**.

LEMON SHARKS often spend time together.

Sharks dive to move to different depths in the ocean. Some sharks, including bull sharks, prefer warm water. They go into deeper or shallower water to find the temperature they like. The **spined pygmy shark** is a small shark that is less than 1 foot long. It lives in deep water during the day and swims to the surface at night to find food.

When a shark becomes an adult, finding a mate and having babies is important. How does a male shark show a female he is interested in her? In many shark species, males bite a female when they want to mate. Female sharks have been found with scars from these bites. In some species, females send out scent signals called pheromones (FER-uh-mohnz). This lets males know that they are interested in mating.

FACT FILE: WORLD TRAVELERS

Many sharks spend time migrating. They travel great distances to find food. Or they migrate to find warmer or cooler waters when seasons change. Some sharks, such as the **sandbar shark**, migrate to find quiet places to give birth. Blue sharks regularly travel from New York to Brazil, a distance of more than 3,500 miles. And salmon sharks travel thousands of miles around the North Pacific, where salmon are found. They migrate to be near their favorite prey.

One great white shark named Nicole migrated more than 12,400 miles. She swam from Southern Africa to Australia and then back again. Her epic journey is the greatest recorded migration by a great white shark. She was named to honor the Australian actress Nicole Kidman, who is devoted to helping sharks and supporting ocean conservation.

Basking sharks are found in the North Atlantic during the warmer months of spring. But where do they go in winter? In 2009, scientists at the Massachusetts Division of Marine Fisheries tagged a group of basking sharks and tracked them using satellites (SA-tuh-lietz). They found out that the sharks traveled all the way to the coast of Brazil. No one knows why basking sharks migrate south for the winter.

DO SHARKS ATTACK? Shark and human encounters are rare . . . except for one hot summer a hundred years ago.

A SHARK BITE STORY

In the summer of 1916, there was an extreme heat wave in the eastern United States. This was before people had air conditioning or backyard pools. Many people went to beaches to cool off. Boat captains reported seeing many sharks that summer, but no one thought much about sharks being near the beach.

Five people at the New Jersey shore were bitten by sharks. Only one survived. These attacks shocked people. They caused a panic across the nation. The New Jersey shark bite story changed the way people thought about sharks. Scientists had spent little time studying sharks until then. After the attacks, they started new research into how and why sharks bite people.

The first bite in the summer of 1916 occurred on Sunday, July 1. A 25-year-old man went swimming with his dog before dinner. He was bitten by a shark. He was rescued by a lifeguard and another swimmer—who said the shark followed them to shore. The man didn't survive the shark bites.

Over the next several days, more shark bites happened. A 27-year-old worker from a local hotel was bitten on the stomach and legs while swimming 130 yards from shore. A rescuer was bitten, too. And a boy playing in Matawan Creek with some friends was pulled under by an 8-foot-long shark. None of these people survived their shark encounters. A half hour after the attack in the creek, another boy was bitten. He survived.

People around the country heard about the shark bites. There was a lot of fear, and beaches up and down the east and west coasts were closed. Some people organized shark hunts. They wanted to kill every shark they could find. People asked the government to protect beaches with nets.

WHICH SHARK WAS RESPONSIBLE?
Scientists have never agreed on which species of shark was responsible for the bites on people. Some medium-size sharks were caught in the area, including a blue shark and a sandbar shark. But scientists said they were probably too small. A young great white shark was found a

Bull shark

Great white shark

few days later, and it became known as the "Jersey Man-Eater." But scientists still debate whether a single young shark was responsible.

Many scientists believe a bull shark was responsible—at least for the attacks in the creek. That's because bull sharks are among the few that can live in fresh water as well as salt water.

The shark bites on the New Jersey shore during the summer of 1916 were rare events. No one knows why they happened. Nothing like it has happened since.

FACT FILE: FACT OR FEAR?

Most of the fear people feel about sharks is not based on facts. When you know the facts, you can see that sharks deserve respect, not fear.

FEAR: Humans are prey for every kind of shark.

FACT: There are about 500 shark species, and only about a dozen have been responsible for most bites on humans. Only four kinds of sharks are of concern to humans because they have bitten people without a reason such as self-defense—bulls, tigers, great whites, and oceanic whitetips.

FEAR: Big sharks want to eat humans.

FACT: Sharks prefer fattier animals, like seals and sea lions. People are too bony. Usually, sharks realize that people aren't the prey they want and they swim away after taking a bite. This is called bite and release.

FEAR: Sharks make the ocean dangerous for humans.

FACT: Sharks kill an average of one person a year in the United States. There are greater dangers at the beach. More than 3,300 people on average die from drowning each year in the United States.

HAPPY HOME A coral reef is home to many different animals.

WHY SHARKS MATTER

Sharks are important. They help keep our oceans healthy and in balance. The number of sharks in the ocean has gone down recently. Many shark species are threatened with extinction. If this happens, they will disappear forever. A healthy ocean provides oxygen, food, water, and good weather. If sharks disappear, the ocean cannot remain healthy.

An ecosystem is a community of creatures that live in a particular

Healthy reef

Dying reef

environment. Some creatures eat other creatures. Some help others. Some take from the environment. Others add to it. All these things happen in a healthy ecosystem.

The oceans of the world are ecosystems that play a major role in life on Earth. Winds that move over the ocean pick up moisture and heat and blow it over the land. This is where much of our weather comes from— including rain. When the oceans are healthy, they provide fresh water for drinking and food for us to eat.

For the ocean ecosystem to remain healthy and to provide all these benefits, the creatures in it must remain in balance.

Sharks are an important part of the ocean ecosystem. They are top predators. This means they eat smaller fish but aren't usually prey themselves. Without

Oceans begin the water cycle.

sharks, or with too few sharks, there would be too many smaller fish. There would not be enough food for all of them and they would start to die off.

Reefs are a good example of how sharks help keep their ecosystem in balance. Reefs form around piles of sand, rocks, or coral growths. They are home to many kinds of ocean life. All kinds of creatures, including sharks, interact on a reef. Small fish eat smaller creatures, such as tiny zooplankton, and algae. Big fish eat smaller fish. Sharks eat many of the bigger fish. If there were no sharks, the bigger fish would eat all the smaller fishes and the algae would grow out of control and damage the reef.

Rather than being afraid of sharks, people should be afraid *for* sharks, because their existence is threatened. The United Nations Food and Agriculture Organization estimates that the populations of almost half of all shark species have seriously shrunk. About one in every five shark species is in danger of disappearing. Scientists think more than 70 million sharks are killed by humans every year. Changes to our climate and pollution have all contributed to the threat.

RESOURCES

There are many good ways to get close to sharks and learn more, including visiting them in an aquarium, watching television shows and series such as Discovery Channel's *Shark Week*, reading books like this one, and joining organizations dedicated to helping sharks.

AQUARIUMS WITH SHARKS

Aquarium of the Pacific
Long Beach, California
aquariumofpacific.org

Audubon Aquarium of
the Americas
New Orleans, Louisiana
*audubonnatureinstitute.
org/aquarium*

Birch Aquarium
La Jolla, California
aquarium.ucsd.edu

Dallas World Aquarium
Dallas, Texas
dwazoo.com

The Florida Aquarium
Tampa, Florida
flaquarium.org

Georgia Aquarium
Atlanta, Georgia
georgiaaquarium.org

The Maritime Aquarium
Norwalk, Connecticut
maritimeaquarium.org

Monterey Bay Aquarium
Monterey, California
montereybayaquarium.org

Mote Marine Laboratory
and Aquarium
Sarasota, Florida
mote.org/aquarium

National Aquarium
Baltimore, Maryland
aqua.org

New England Aquarium
Boston, Massachusetts
neaq.org

Newport Aquarium
Newport, Kentucky
newportaquarium.com

New York Aquarium
Brooklyn, New York
nyaquarium.com

Pittsburgh Zoo & PPG
Aquarium
Pittsburgh, Pennsylvania
pittsburghzoo.org

Shedd
Aquarium
Chicago,
Illinois
sheddaquarium.org

Steinhart Aquarium
San Francisco, California
*calacademy.org/exhibits/
steinhart-aquarium*

Tennessee Aquarium
Chattanooga, Tennessee
tnaqua.org

ORGANIZATIONS

The Shark Foundation
shark.ch/index.html

Shark Project
sharkproject.org/en

Shark Savers
sharksavers.org

The Shark Trust
sharktrust.org

BOOKS

The Big Book of Sharks,
by the Discovery Channel
(Discovery/Time)

*Discovery Channel
Sharkopedia: The
Complete Guide to
Everything Shark,*
(Discovery/Time)

Sharks of the World, by
Leonardo Compagno,
Marc Dando, and Sarah
Fowler (Princeton
University Press, 2005)

MEET THE SHARK ORDERS

Scientists have divided all the sharks in the world into eight groups called orders. Sharks in each order have similar features. Within each order, the sharks are divided into families, which have even more similar features. Within each family, there are species; there is only one type of shark in each species.

ANGELSHARKS: 18 species in one family

CARPETSHARKS: 42 species in seven families, including bamboo shark, nurse shark, whale shark, wobbegong, and zebra shark

DOGFISH SHARKS: 120 species in seven families, including Greenland shark, dwarf lanternshark, green lanternshark, lanternshark, ninja lanternshark, smalleye pygmy shark, spined pygmy shark, and spiny dogfish shark

FRILLED SHARKS AND COWSHARKS: 6 species in two families, including frilled shark, sevengill shark, and sixgill shark

HORN AND BULLHEAD SHARKS: 9 species in one family, including bullhead shark, horn shark, and Port Jackson shark

MACKEREL SHARKS: 15 species in seven families, including basking shark, common thresher shark, goblin shark, great white shark, mako shark, porbeagle shark, salmon shark, sand tiger shark, shortfin mako shark, and thresher shark

SAWSHARKS: 10 species in one family

GROUNDSHARKS: There are many species in the groundshark order; they are grouped into the five categories below.

Catsharks: 154 species in three families, including catshark, chain catshark, Galápagos catshark, leopard catshark, pajama shark or striped catshark, pale catshark, Panama ghost catshark, puffadder shyshark, and swell shark

Hammerhead sharks: 9 species in one family, including great hammerhead shark and scalloped hammerhead shark

Houndsharks: 47 species in two families, including leopard shark, smoothhound shark, tope shark, and whiskery shark

Requiem sharks: 54 species in one family, including blacktip shark, blue shark, bull shark, Caribbean reef shark, lemon shark, oceanic whitetip shark, sandbar shark, silky shark, spinner shark, and tiger shark

Weasel sharks: 8 species in one family, including Atlantic weasel shark, Australian weasel shark, and snaggletooth shark

INDEX

Illustrations are indicated by **boldface**. When they fall within a page span, the entire span is **boldface**.

A

Angelsharks 15, **15,** 48–50, **50,** 56, 110

B

Baby sharks **58,** 58–65, **61**
Bamboo sharks 62, 70, **70,** 110
Basking sharks 75, **75,** 93, 110
Biting and attacking 31, 45, 63, 91, 94–101
Blue sharks 40, 65, 92, 98, 110
Bodies and features **4–6,** 4–15, **10–11, 14–15,** 28–29, **28–29, 68,** 68–81, **70–72, 75, 78, 81**
Breaching 34–35, **35**
Breathing 9–10, 56–57, 87–88
Bullhead sharks 40, 60, 72–73, 110
Bull sharks 13, 16, **16,** 45, 90–91, **98,** 99, 100, 110

C

Caribbean reef sharks 4, **4–5,** 110
Catsharks 51–53, 67, 77, 110
Coral reefs 102, **102, 104,** 104–106

D

Differences in sharks **4–6,** 4–15, **10–11, 14–15,** 64–67, **66–67,** 85
Dogfish sharks 12, 47–48, **48,** 61, **61,** 110

E

Egg laying 58, **58,** 60–62, **61**
Electrical signals (electroreception) 17–18, **22,** 22–23, 79–80, 88
Eyesight and eyes **5,** 13, 15, **15,** 18–20, **19,** 28, **28,** 31–32, 51, **78,** 79–80, **81**

F

Fins **4–6,** 10–12, **11,** 87, 89, **94**
Food and feeding habits 8, 13, 18, 23–32, **34–36,** 34–45, **38–39,** 47–54, 62–63, 68, **68,** 74–75, **75,** 84–85, 100–101, 105
Frilled sharks 72, 110

G

Galápagos catsharks 77, 110
Gills **5,** 9–10, **10–11,** 40, 56, 72, 87
Goblin sharks 74, 110

H

Great white sharks **26,** 26–35, **28–29, 35,** 40–41, 66, **66–67, 88,** 88–89, 92, 98–99, **99,** 100, 110
Greenland sharks 65–66, **66–67,** 110

H

Hammerhead sharks (smart sharks) 15, **15,** 65, 66, **66–67, 78,** 78–85, **81–83,** 89, 110
Hearing and ears 20–21
Horn sharks 61, **61,** 62, **72,** 72–73, 110
Hunting habits 8, 13, 18, 23–32, **34–36,** 34–45, **38–39,** 47–54, 62–63, 68, **68,** 74–75, **75,** 84–85, 100–101, 105

I

Importance of sharks 102–107

J

Jaws and mouths 5, **5,** 9, 26, **26,** 32, 37, 42, 49, 63, 74, 78, **78**

L

Lantern sharks 14, **14,** 67, 73–74, 110
Lemon sharks 14, **14,** 61, **61,** 90, **90,** 110
Leopard sharks 24–25, **25,** 53, 110
Lifespans 64–65

M

Mako sharks 13–14, **14, 40,** 44, **44,** 52, 110
Mating 73, 85, 89, 91
Migration habits 33, 92–93, **93**

N

Nurse sharks 12, 42, 46, **46,** 56–57, **57,** 110

O

Ocean ecosystems **102,** 102–107, **104**
Oceanic whitetip sharks 10, 12, 90, 100, 110
Odd sharks **68,** 68–77, **70–72, 75**

P

Pajama sharks 53, 110
Porbeagle sharks 65, 110
Puffadder shysharks 52–53, 110

R

Remoras 86, **86**

S

Salmon sharks 12, 52, 92, 110
Sandbar sharks 92, 98, 110
Sawsharks 68, **68,** 110
Scientific studies 12, 24–25, 31, 33, 76–77, 84, 93, 96–99
Senses 17–25, **19, 22**
Sevengill sharks 90, 110
Silky sharks 90, 110
Sixgill sharks 62–63, 110
Skin 8, 13, 28–29, **28–29,** 63, 69–71, **70–71,** 75–77
Smalleye pygmy sharks 67, 110
Smelling and snouts **5,** 18, 24–25, 28, 32, 45, 51, 68, **68,** 74, 91
Smoothhound sharks 64, 110
Social habits and communication 87–91
Species of sharks 7, 74, 76–77, 80–81, 100, 110
Spined pygmy sharks 91, 110
Spinner sharks 53, 110
Spiny dogfish sharks 47–48, **48,** 110
Submersible vessels 76–77, **77**
Survival and protection skills **28–29,** 28–30, 32, 37, 45, **45,** 60, 62–64, 68–74, **70–71,** 84–85
Swell sharks 51–52, 110
Swimming and movement 10–11, 31, 34–35, **35,** 47–53, **82–83,** 82–85, 87–91, **90**

T

Tails **4,** 12, 48, **48,** 52–55, **55,** 70
Tasting sense 21, 23
Teeth **5,** 9, **26, 28–30,** 29–31, 37, **39,** 39–43, **41,** 49, 53, 63, 72, 74–75, **75,** 78
Threats to sharks 12, 96, 102–107
Thresher sharks 54–55, **54–55,** 66, **66–67,** 110
Tiger sharks 6, **6,** 13, 19, **19,** 45, 60, 100, 110
Touching sense 21

W

Water cycle 104–105, **105**
Whale sharks 14, **14,** 38, **38–39,** 64, 65, 66, **66–67,** 110
Wobbegongs **45,** 56, 71, **71,** 110

Z

Zebra sharks 15, **15,** 110

CREDITS AND ACKNOWLEDGMENTS

Writer Lori Stein
Produced by Scout Books & Media Inc
President and Project Director Susan Knopf
Project Manager Brittany Gialanella
Copyeditor Beth Adelman, Michael Centore
Proofreader Chelsea Burris
Designer Annemarie Redmond
Advisor Andy Dehart
VP of Animal Husbandry, Patricia and Phillip Frost Museum of Science

Thanks to the Time Inc. Books team: Margot Schupf, Anja Schmidt, Beth Sutinis, Deirdre Langeland, Georgia Morrissey, Megan Pearlman, Melodie George, and Sue Chodakiewicz.

Special thanks to the Discovery and Animal Planet Creative and Licensing Teams: Denny Chen, Tracy Conner, Elizabeta Ealy, Robert Marick, Doris Miller, Sue Perez-Jackson, and Janet Tsuei.

PHOTO CREDITS

Key: SS – Shutterstock; DT – Dreamstime; GY – Getty; NPL – naturepl.com; IS – iStock
TtB: Top to bottom; LtR: Left to right
FRONT COVER: ©vladoskan/IS
p. 1: ©vladoskan/IS; p. 3: ©Vincent Canabal/Discovery Communications, LLC; pp. 4-5: ©Michael Bogner/DT; p. 6: ©Liquid Productions, LLC/SS; pp. 10-11: ©Predrag Vuckovic/IS; p. 14 TtB: ©Greg Amptman/SS, ©nicolasvoisin44/SS; p. 15 TtB: ©SeraphP/SS, ©Royalty-Free/Corbis/Discovery Communications, LLC, ©Pvb969924/DT, ©kaschibo/SS; p. 16: ©Fiona Ayerst/DT; p. 19 LtR: ©rkankaro/IS, ©Birgul Ozbek Erken/IS; p. 22: ©Brandelet/S0053; p. 25: ©David Litman/SS; p. 26: ©Reinhard Dirscheri/GY; pp. 28-29: ©Chris Fallows/Discovery Communications, LLC; p. 30 LtR: ©Mark Kostich/IS, ©Joe_Potato/IS; p. 35: ©Chris Fallows/Discovery Communications, LLC; p. 36: ©A Cotton Photo/SS; pp. 38-39: ©mihtiander/IS; p. 41: ©IMNATURE/IS; pp. 44-45 LtR: ©NOAA, ©Ethan Daniels/SS; p. 46: ©NOAA; p. 48: ©NOAA/CBNMS; p. 50: ©Kelvin Aitken-V&W/ASSOCIATED PRESS; pp. 54-55: ©nicolasvoisin44/SS; p. 57: ©Subsurface/DT; p. 58: ©Andrea Izzotti/IS; p. 61 TtB: ©Doug Perrine/NPL, ©BMCL/SS, ©Moment Open/GY; pp. 62-63: ©Maxim Catana/SS; pp. 66-67 TtB: ©Ethan Daniels/SS, ©SeaPics.com, ©Chris Fallows/Discovery Communications, LLC, ©nicolasvoisin44/SS, ©Derek Heasley/SS; p. 68: ©SeaPics; p. 70-71 LtR: ©Barcroft Media/GY, ©Mathieu Meur/Stocktreck Images/GY; p. 72: ©Irko Van Der Heide/DT; p. 75: ©Oxford Scientific/GY; p. 77: ©NOAA; p. 78: ©Tomas Kotouc/SS; p. 81 CL: ©Gerard Soury/GY, ©Frhojdysz/DT, ©Chris & Monique Fallows/NPL; pp. 82-83: ©Tomas Kotouc/SS; p. 86: ©Soren Egeberg/DT; pp. 88-89: ©Willyam Bradberry/SS; p. 90: ©Fiona Ayerst/DT; p. 93: ©AridOcean/SS; p. 94: ©Jamen Percy/SS; pp. 98-99 LtR: ©ShaneGross/IS, ©Thurston Photo/IS; p. 101: ©karen roach/SS; p. 102: ©frantisekhojdysz/SS; pp. 104-105 LtR: ©Parnupong Norasethkamol/DT, ©Ethan Daniels/SS, ©Elena Torre/DT; p. 107: ©Milena Moiola/DT